HOW TO

INCREASE PROFIT

MARGIN IN THE FOOTWEAR

INDUSTRY IN

5

EASY STEPS

HOW TO

INCREASE PROFIT MARGIN IN THE FOOTWEAR INDUSTRY IN 5 EASY STEPS

Dr. DEEPIKA SINGHAL RAHUL SINGHAL

Printing & Packaging Strategists

Worldwide Published by

Pendown Press

PENDOWN PRESS

An ISO 9001 & ISO 14001 Certified Co.,
Regd. Office: 2525/193, 1st Floor, Onkar Nagar-A,
Tri Nagar, Delhi-110035
Ph.: 09350849407, 09312235086
E-mail: info@pendownpress.com
Branch Office: 1A/2A, 20, Hari Sadan, Ansari Road,
Daryaganj, New Delhi-110002
Ph.: 011-45794768
Website: PendownPress.com

First Edition: 2022

ISBN: 978-93-5554-124-6

*To all my fellow
Business Owners who
Love Innovation
and
Love Packaging*

*This book is dedicated
to You!*

Contents

Who Is This Book For?

We have written this book to guide all footwear manufacturers who want to skyrocket their profits and become leading names in the industry. By the end of this book, you will gain significant breakthroughs and experience several **A-HA! moments** that will lead you to strategic planning, cost reduction and profit maximization - that's our promise.

Why This Book?

As a doctor and engineer, our relationship with our customers has always been more than a fiduciary one. Our customers deserve the very best in their business. If we fail to live up to their expectations, we feel that the purpose of our life will remain unfulfilled.

While planning for the conclave, we realized that when we present in the conclave, it can sometimes be very overwhelming and why not have a handbook for our dear guests. We wanted to ensure that any footwear manufacturer, independent of whether they are our customer, deserves a good guide because the proper knowledge in this field will pave the way for a healthy future.

The very purpose of writing this book is to create awareness with our readers how the profit margins can be increased in their business, just by looking at some key but neglected areas and other relevant topics.

We encourage you to read every chapter. Also learn how to do things correctly, as the right actions will achieve the desired outcomes.

How To Use This Book?

This book is in your hands because you have good reason to believe that by reading this book, you will be able to alleviate your profit margins to a large extent. And the purpose of writing this book is to live up to that expectation.

Before you start reading the book, We would like to give you some tips regarding the better use of this book:

- **Read the book in sequence:** We have seen readers thumbing through the pages, concentrating on a few topics. They choose to read only those topics or chapters that are related to themselves or their dear ones; however it is important to read the entire book in sequence. Reading it in this fashion will provide you with a comprehensive view of the subject matter.

- **Focus your attention on tips:** The tips mentioned at the end of every chapter are practical and doable action points.

- **Conclusion:** By reading all the chapters, you may feel like you need not read the 'conclusion', however don't make the mistake of omitting it. The conclusion carries all the essentials that we have discussed, things to be taken into consideration, and practiced.

We are very optimistic that the above-mentioned suggestions will help you extract the maximum value out of this book.

Foreword

Prof. (Dr.) Sanjay Gupta

BTech, PhD (IIT Delhi)
Vice Chancellor, World University of Design Sonipat

Packaging Design as an area of intervention has not attracted as much attention in India as it should have. In a retail environment, product packaging design plays the most important role of branding a product, communicating the product's personality or function, and generating a sale. The 'catchier' the design, the more audiences it will attract. A good design differentiates the products from its competitors, captures attention from the shelf and draw the customers in. Packaging can alter perceptions of customers about the value of the product.

But packaging design is not just visual attraction. Packaging protects the product from damage, it informs, provide hygiene and acts as a preventive measure. Packaging also saves costs in shipping, transportation, and storage etc. Packaging can also send a message that you care about the environment and can provide a CSR option.

There's so much one can do with packaging design. I am therefore so happy that Dr. Deepika and Rahul Singhal decided to write this book, extracting learnings from 23 years of their rich experience of providing packaging solutions and strategies to footwear manufacturing industry.

As packaging partners, they have found solutions to multiple challenges footwear manufacturers face. They have managed to build packaging design into the strategic planning of these companies thereby ensuring not only cost reduction but profit maximization. The tools and techniques developed by them to help footwear manufacturers will no doubt help all readers of the book.

I hope this book proves to be a game-changer for the multitude of footwear brands and for this industry.

Acknowledgements

We would like to express our gratitude to the people who helped us complete this book to its current form; to all those who provided support, talked things over, read, revised, offered comments, allowed us to quote their remarks, and assisted in editing, proofreading and design.

First and foremost, we would like to thank our parents, Mrs. Prabha Singhal and Mr. BP Jain who gave us abundant love and nurturing environment during our childhood years. That enabled us to be self-confident and independent.

We want to thank Shreeya, Diya, Khushi and Aanya for keeping us energized at all phases of writing this book.

Most importantly, we would like to thank the main driving force behind this book – our Marketing mentor and now our life coach, Akshar Yadav, without whose push and drive this book would not have come into existence. The list of acknowledgements will be incomplete without mentioning our business partners, team of Packaging India and customers who have supported and guided us in this journey. We cannot thank you enough for the contributions you have made to our life and business.

It would be incomplete not to mention what Mr. NK Aggarwal, Mr. RK Gupta from Action shoes, Mr. HK Aggarwal from Campus shoes, Mr. Ramesh Dua of Relaxo, Mr. V. Naushad of Walkaroo, have done for us and guided us on every step.

Special thanks to Mr. Subodh Gupta of Microtek for lighting the drive to do something innovative.

We are really very thankful to Dinesh Verma, CEO, Pendown Press and his team for their support and suggestion during the creative process.

Last but not the least, we beg forgiveness of all those who have been with us over the years and whose names we have failed to mention.

Develop New And Better Footwear Designs

Designs are the soul of your footwear business. Want to become your customers' first and only choice? Then focus on selling footwear that ranks high on creativity, concept, and innovation.

The FDDI has set up a center of excellence at Rohtak, which will work closely with you on your development & design. They will charge a nominal fee on some of the most successful & latest hi-tech machines from China, France and Italy. These machines execute your creative ideas, design references, and smart prints and provide valuable support in the Indian context, helping you make your footwear designs bestsellers.

Believe it or not, the first thing a customer notices and admires about your footwear products is their overall look, beauty and comfort. Augment visual appeal. Only then do they move on to checking other aspects of quality.

Hence, to increase the retail sales of your footwear business, invest in world-class photoshoots for each of your products so that you can capture and showcase the beauty and charm of your products.

Currently, many reputed brands are associated with Packaging India and are reaping the benefits of having an industry expert by their side.

Tip

Create a special, niche collection of your footwear to help you skyrocket your sales. Don't just tell your customers your products are awesome; show them with the help of imagery.

– STEP 2 –

Magic Of New And Better Materials

There are numerous new and better materials available in the market. Experimenting with newer materials, colors, styles, etc., will catch the fancy of young and trendy buyers. The moment you attract the attention of your end customer, half of the sale process is done. You will provide exclusivity over other manufacturers that will give you the edge. Some of these new materials are even more environmentally friendly, wear-resistant, sustainable, and comfortable.

The packaging products made by Packaging India are the result of using R&D along with new technology, and the same principles, when applied to footwear manufacturing, will definitely boost sales.

Tip

Hire a more professional team who can keep your R&D for better products at full steam. The Government of India is providing full support for this purpose to the industry.

3

New Channels To Sell At Higher Margins And Assured Timely Payments

Do you know what is the latest happening in sales?

Do you want your customers to connect to your brand directly and pay you directly too – in advance/before delivery of material to them?

Think about the last time you purchased a new mobile phone. Did you just go and buy from a mobile store straightaway? You will probably say "no". There is a great chance you researched the various models available online, compared many models and then decided on what you want to buy. It is possible that you decided to buy the phone from a store or you ordered it online.

You got the delivery at the comfort of your home, and that too at a discounted price compared to the store. So this shows the importance of being present online, and if this is valid for a mobile phone of such high value, it is possible for footwear too. The moment the end customer (read it as your retailers) reaches you directly, you can provide them with a discount because you have eliminated the extra channels where you often have to spend money. This customer/retailers gives you instant payment, and you dispatch the material. Or you dispatch the material first, and then the moment the customer takes the delivery, you get the payment.

- Can you think of any payment terms better than these?

- Can you imagine profits better than these?

- Can you get better feedback than this?

You know what the customer likes or doesn't like every day. With this instant feedback, your production schedule doesn't have to wait for what the distributor says.

The only restriction in your mind might be about the volumes such sales can bring. But you'd be surprised to know that some brands have as much as 40% sales in this format presently? There are even a number of players currently who are selling only online. And they are doing really well.

You can also cross-sell or upsell your products easily online, which will surely increase your profits.

Tip

Make online sales the primary focus of your retail strategy. Make upselling and cross-selling a significant part of your retail sales strategy, and watch your profits multiply.

Focus On Quality/Care

Maintaining the quality of your product is of paramount importance. By selling high-quality footwear, you can gain the trust and win the hearts of your customers.

When this happens, your customers always return to you and buy from you. They recommend your brand to their family and friends, leading to windfall sales and repeat customers. That's why you should pay attention to quality certifications while designing your product.

Tip

Consistently work towards enhancing the quality of your products, and you will never be short of customers.

– STEP 5 –

Stay Updated With The Latest Trends

You would all agree that Packaging is the face of your product. To know what best suits your product, always source your packaging from trustworthy and reliable partners who are in touch with the latest trends in the local and global markets.

Find out what styles, colors and designs of Footwear Packaging are the most popular among consumers and other manufacturers. Stay updated with the ongoing trends, and you will ensure that your customers are happy with your brand and the variety of footwear you offer with utmost comfort.

Footwear Manufacturers who have been associated with Packaging India as their packaging partner have taken the benefit of the patented QSTCL framework and have recorded significant growth in their sales by focusing on what they need to focus on, not what their partners need to focus on, in packaging.

Tip

Always keep a finger on the pulse of your industry if you want to stand out from the competition and be the preferred choice of your customers.

7

Closing Thoughts

The five techniques we have mentioned in this book are based on our successful tenure running Packaging India and making it North India's Fastest growing 3 Ply Multicoloured Corrugated Box Brand for Premium Brands.

By adding innovative designs to your portfolio, showcasing the look of your products, selling online, cross-selling and up-selling, focusing on quality and staying updated with the latest market trends, you can skyrocket your footwear sales within just a few weeks.

We urge you to try them now and see the difference they make to your sales figures and profit margins.

Now You have 2 choices, either you continue with whatever type of packaging you are using.

OR

You can choose to have expert personal guidance to overcome all your challenges and sail smoothly toward profitability.

Go to Deepikarahul.com/interest.

Get a comprehensive audit of your packaging needs worth Rs. 1,28,000/- + 18% GST for Free and tips to have a cost-effective multicolour printed packaging.

Go to Deepikarahul.com/audit.

Connect with us at:

Email–rs@packagingindia.in

www.linkedin.com/in/dr-deepika-singhal-packaging-india

www.linkedin.com/in/rahul-singhal-packaging-india/

9 789355 541246